1ST GRADE PHONICS
Unit 9
Spelling Ending Sounds

MW01593560

TABLE OF CONTENTS

IMPORTANT: Please refer to the Teacher Guide for specific scripts, procedures, and words that are represented by pictures.

Throughout this Unit, learners will scan QR codes. Be careful they scan each code individually.

LEARN

- Spelling words with silent final **e**
- Spelling words with **dge** and **tch**
- Spelling words with suffixes

DAILY PAGE GOALS

Day	Complete	Day	Complete	Day	Complete
1	ii–7	7	35–42	13	70–76
2	8–15	8	43–50	14	77–84
3	16–22	9	51–58	15	85–91
4	23–28	10	59–63	16	92–96
5	29–30	11	64–65	17	97–98
6	31–34	12	66–69	18	99–102

Teacher reads all pages to the learners.

1. SPELLING LIST 13: Part 1

Learn:

- Read words that end with **se**.
- Spell and read words from List 13.

WRITING PHONOGRAM REVIEW

 **Listen to and write the phonograms.**
Underline any multi-letter phonograms.

WORKING WITH WORDS

The words in List 13 end with a silent final **e**. The silent final **e** has many jobs. Its main job is to be the "Vowel Boss." It makes vowels say their long sounds.

For List 13, you will learn about the other jobs of silent final **e**.

Silent Final e Job: Suffix Stopper

Stops phonograms from looking like suffixes

moose   moos

 # Write the correct answers.
Sort the words under the correct pictures.

horse	nurse	mouse
house	goose	cheese

1)

2)

3)

4)

5)

6)

Listen!

? **Circle the correct answers.**

7) | syllables | 1 | 2 | 3 | 4 |

8) | sounds | 1 | 2 | 3 | 4 |

✏️ **Write and read.**

9) _____

? **Choose the correct answer.**

10) The vowel sound is ____.
- ○ r-controlled
- ○ short
- ○ long

Listen!

 **Circle the correct answers.**

11)	syllables	1	2	3	4

12)	sounds	1	2	3	4

 **Write and read.**

13) _____

 **Choose the correct answer.**

14) Which position is the vowel sound in?
   - ○ beginning
   - ○ middle
   - ○ ending

Listen!

? Circle the correct answers.

15)	syllables	1	2	3	4

16)	sounds	1	2	3	4

✏️ Write and read.

17) _____

? Choose the correct answer.

18) What is the syllable type?
- ○ vowel team
- ○ open
- ○ r-controlled

 **Choose the correct answer.**

19) Why do the words *please*, *choose*, and *noise* end with a silent final **e**?

○ to stop the letter **s** from looking like a suffix
○ to make the vowel sounds long
○ to show that the words are plural

 **Write the correct answers.**
Complete the sentences.

| please | choose | noise |

20) It was hard to _____ a new toy.

21) I picked a drum set that makes a lot of _____.

22) May I _____ go play with it?

SCORE ○   CORRECT ○   RESCORE ○

Learn:

- Write sentences using words with a silent final **e**.

- Spell and read words from List 13.

WRITING PHONOGRAM REVIEW

 **Listen to and write the phonograms.**
Underline any multi-letter phonograms.

WORKING WITH WORDS

Keeps the records of words from other languages and from a long time ago

no**n**e

go**n**e

co**m**e

 **Write the correct answers.**
Use the pictures to help you read the words. Then,
use each word in a sentence.

1)

axe

2)

one

3)

giraffe

Listen!

 **Circle the correct answers.**

4)	syllables	1	2	3	4

5)	sounds	1	2	3	4

 **Write and read.**

6) _____

 **Choose the correct answer.**

7) What is the syllable type?
- ○ r-controlled
- ○ vowel team
- ○ VCe

Listen!

 **Circle the correct answers.**

| 8) | syllables | 1 | 2 | 3 | 4 |

| 9) | sounds | 1 | 2 | 3 | 4 |

 **Write and read.**

10) _____

 **Choose the correct answer.**

11) The vowel sound is ____.
  ○ short
  ○ long
  ○ r-controlled

Listen!

 **Circle the correct answers.**

| 12) | syllables | 1 | 2 | 3 | 4 |

| 13) | sounds | 1 | 2 | 3 | 4 |

 **Write and read.**

14) _____

 **Choose the correct answer.**

15) Which reading rule does this word follow?

○ **o** before **m**, **n**, or **v**

○ 1st sound of **oo**

○ 3rd sound of **u**

Listen!

 **Circle the correct answers.**

16)	syllables	1	2	3	4

17)	sounds	1	2	3	4

 **Write and read.**

18) _____

 **Choose the correct answers.**

19) Mark (☒) TWO reading rules that this word follows.

☐ **o** before **m**, **n**, or **v**

☐ beginning **s**

☐ 3rd sound of **u**

? Choose the correct answer.

20) Which word begins with a vowel sound?

    ○ are   ○ some   ○ were

 ## Write the correct answers.
Sort the words in ABC order.

are	were	done

21) _____

22) _____

23) _____

 ## Use the word in your own sentence.

some

24) _____

Learn:

- Read and sort words by their ending letters.
- Spell and read words from List 13.

WRITING PHONOGRAM REVIEW

 **Listen to and write the phonograms.**
Underline any multi-letter phonograms.

WORKING WITH WORDS

Silent Final **e** Job: VZ Saver

Saves the letters **v** and **z** from being the last letter in a word

car**ve** free**ze**

Silent Final **e** Job: CG Softener

Softens the sounds of the letters **c** and **g**

choi**ce** oran**ge**

Write the correct answers.
Read and sort the words by the ending letters.

large	dance	breeze	juice
have	sneeze	sponge	weave

1) ve

2) ze

3) ce

4) ge

Listen!

 **Circle the correct answers.**

5)	syllables	1	2	3	4

6)	sounds	1	2	3	4

 **Write and read.**

7) _____

 **Choose the correct answer.**

8) Why does the word end with a silent final **e**?
   ○ to soften the letter **g**
   ○ to save **v** from being the last letter
   ○ to make the vowel sound long

Listen!

? **Circle the correct answers.**

| 9) | syllables | 1 | 2 | 3 | 4 |

| 10) | sounds | 1 | 2 | 3 | 4 |

Write and read.

11) _____

? **Choose the correct answer.**

12) The vowel sound is ____.
   ○ short
   ○ r-controlled
   ○ long

Listen!

 **Circle the correct answers.**

13)	syllables	1	2	3	4

14)	sounds	1	2	3	4

 **Write and read.**

15) _____

 **Choose the correct answer.**

16) Why does the word end with a silent final **e**?
- ○ to save **z** from being the last letter
- ○ to make the vowel sound long
- ○ to soften the letter **c**

 **Choose the correct answers.**

17) Mark (☒) TWO words that have vowel teams.

☐ leave

☐ give

☐ voice

 **Write the correct answers.**
Complete the sentences.

voice	give	leave

18) It is time to _____ the park.

19) I need to _____ this ball back to Chance.

20) I will follow the sound of his _____.

SCORE   CORRECT   RESCORE

PHONOGRAM REVIEW

 **Listen to and circle the correct phonograms.**

1)  igh   oe   ay

2)  ui   oo   o

3)  p   t   b

4)  ch   qu   k

5)  ph   wh   sh

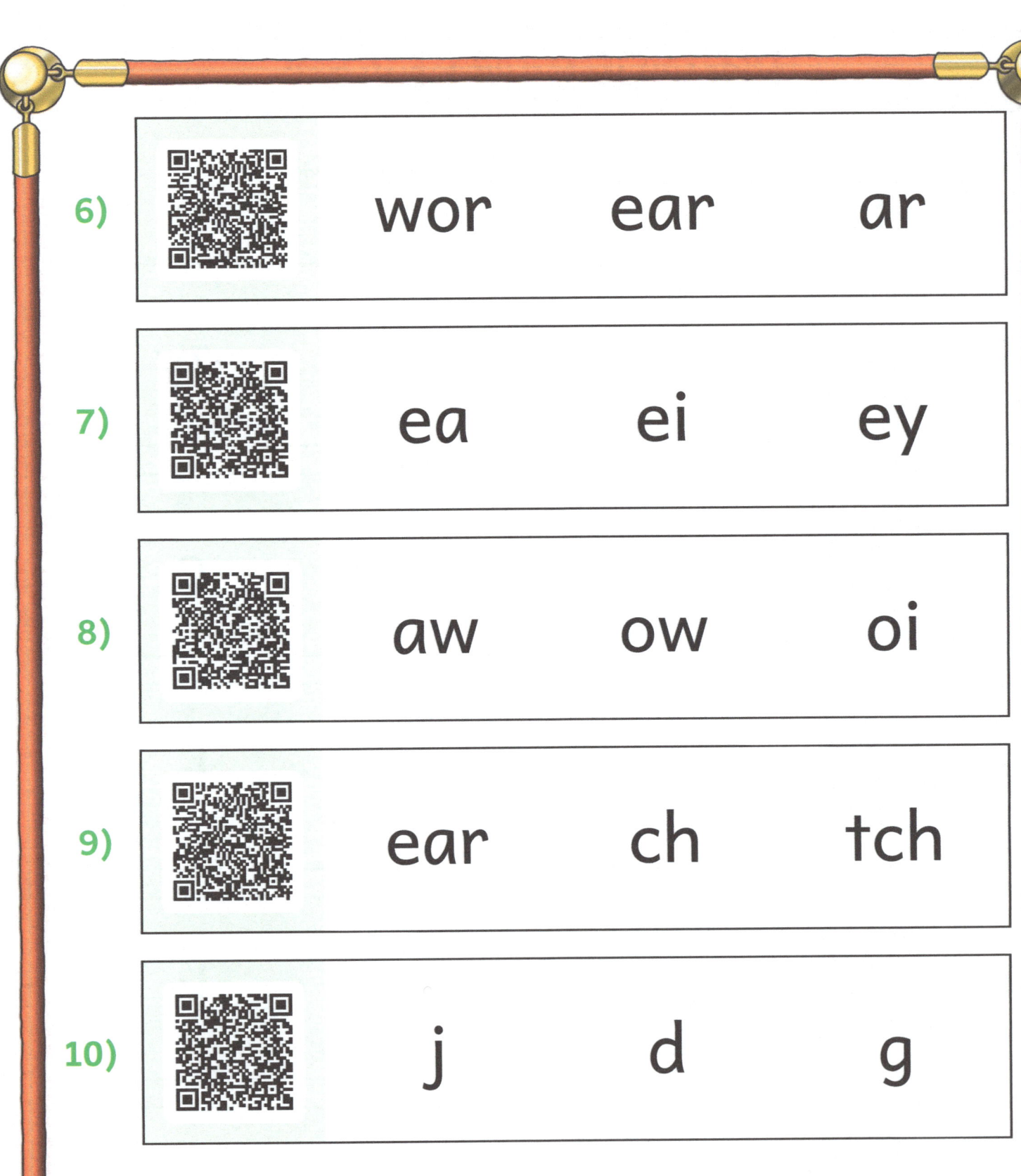

6) wor   ear   ar

7) ea   ei   ey

8) aw   ow   oi

9) ear   ch   tch

10) j   d   g

11)	ng	nk	th
12)	j	g	dge
13)	eigh	ey	ough
14)	e	ai	a
15)	l	t	b

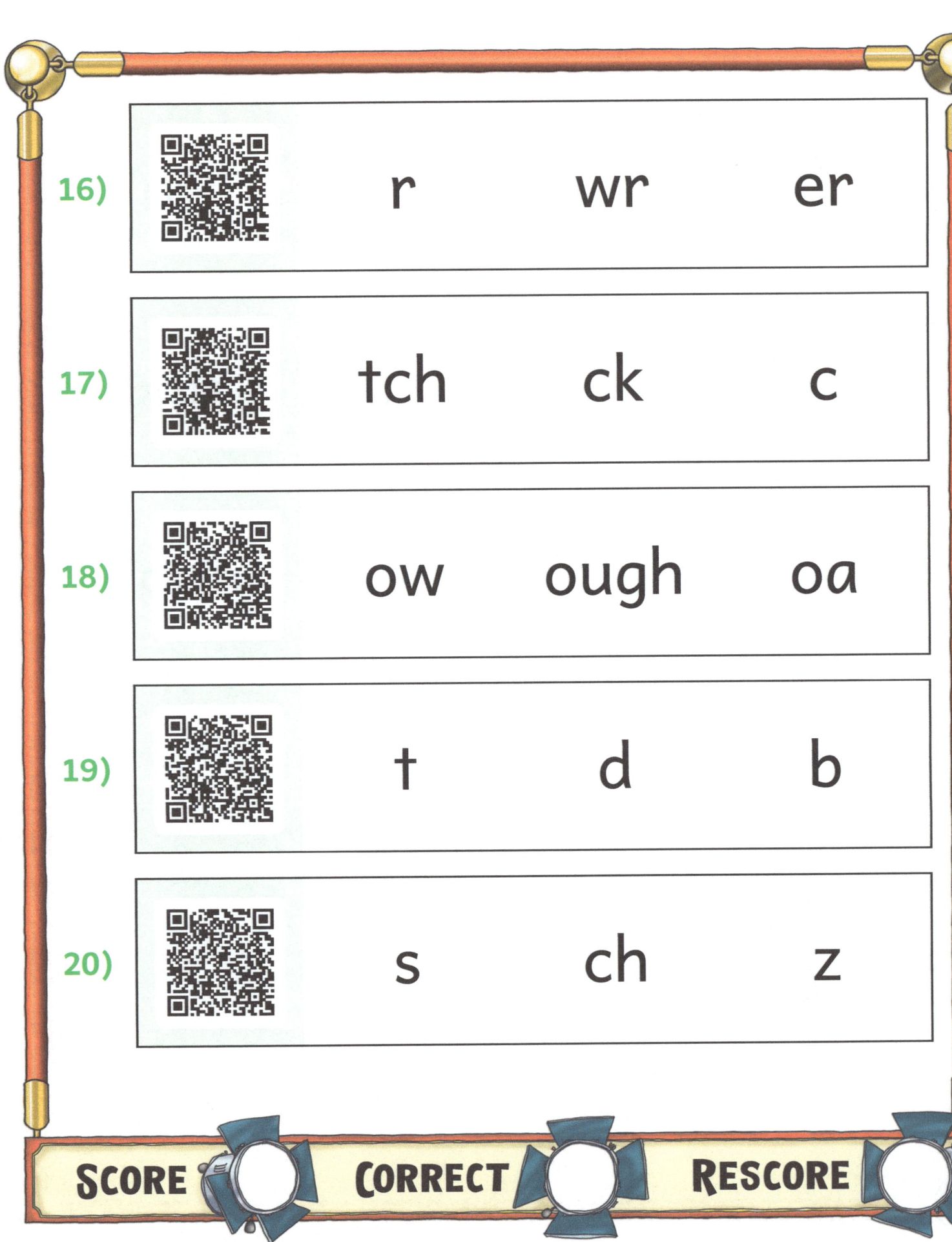

16) r   wr   er

17) tch   ck   c

18) ow   ough   oa

19) t   d   b

20) s   ch   z

SCORE   CORRECT   RESCORE

 **Listen to and circle the correct words.**

1)  voice   noise   choose

2)  give   are   were

3)  some   done   give

4)  done   choose   some

5)  noise   please   voice

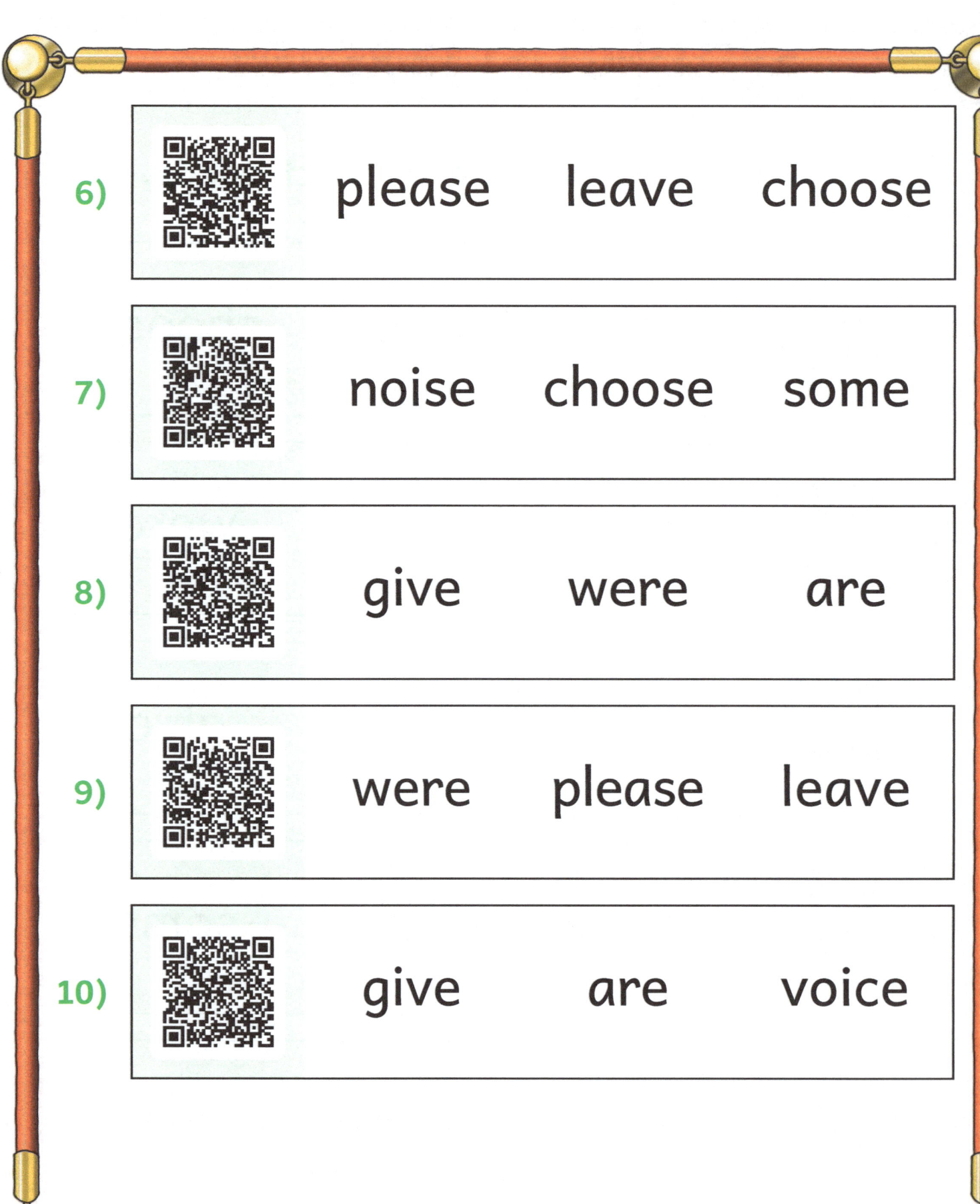

6) please leave choose

7) noise choose some

8) give were are

9) were please leave

10) give are voice

READER 20: "Tug Finds His Voice"

Before you read, practice these words.

Read	Trace	Read	Trace
here	here	noise	noise
are	are	give	give
some	some	bye	bye
dance	dance	were	were
voice	voice	loose	loose
beehive	beehive	done	done

Time to Read!

Reader 20

Tug Finds His Voice

 **Choose the correct answers.**

1) What is one thing Tug can do?
   - ○ play drums
   - ○ dance
   - ○ tell jokes

2) What does Tug say he cannot do?
   - ○ sing
   - ○ jump
   - ○ draw

3) What does Tug's singing voice sound like?
   - ○ *chirp*
   - ○ *woof*
   - ○ *buzz*

4) What helps Tug realize he can sing?
   - ○ the birds
   - ○ the bees
   - ○ the beach

Phonogram Test 25

Listen to and write the correct phonograms.
Underline any multi-letter phonograms.

1)

2)

3)

4)

5)

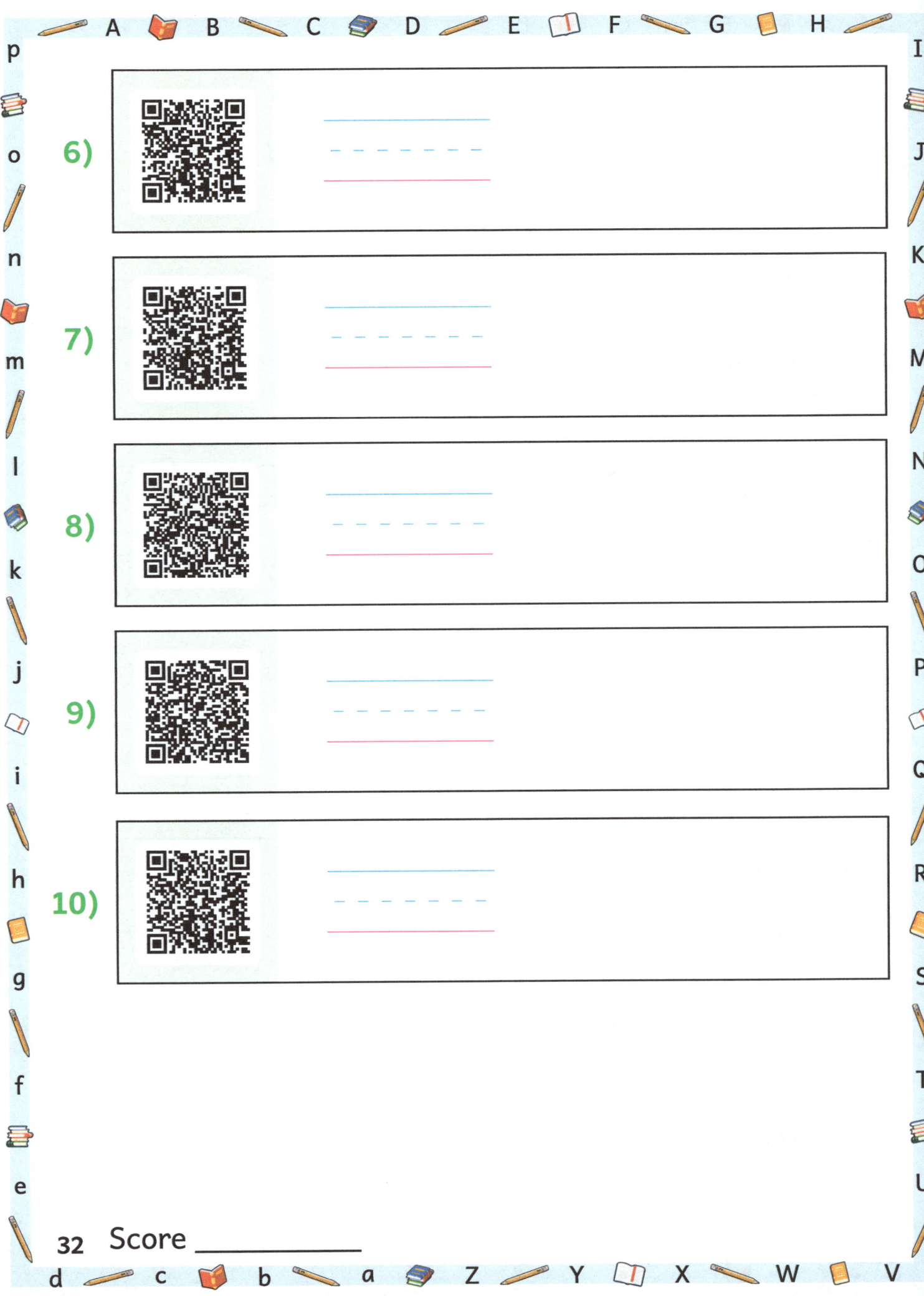

6)

7)

8)

9)

10)

Score _____

Spelling Test List 13

Listen to and write the spelling words.

1)

2)

3)

4)

5)

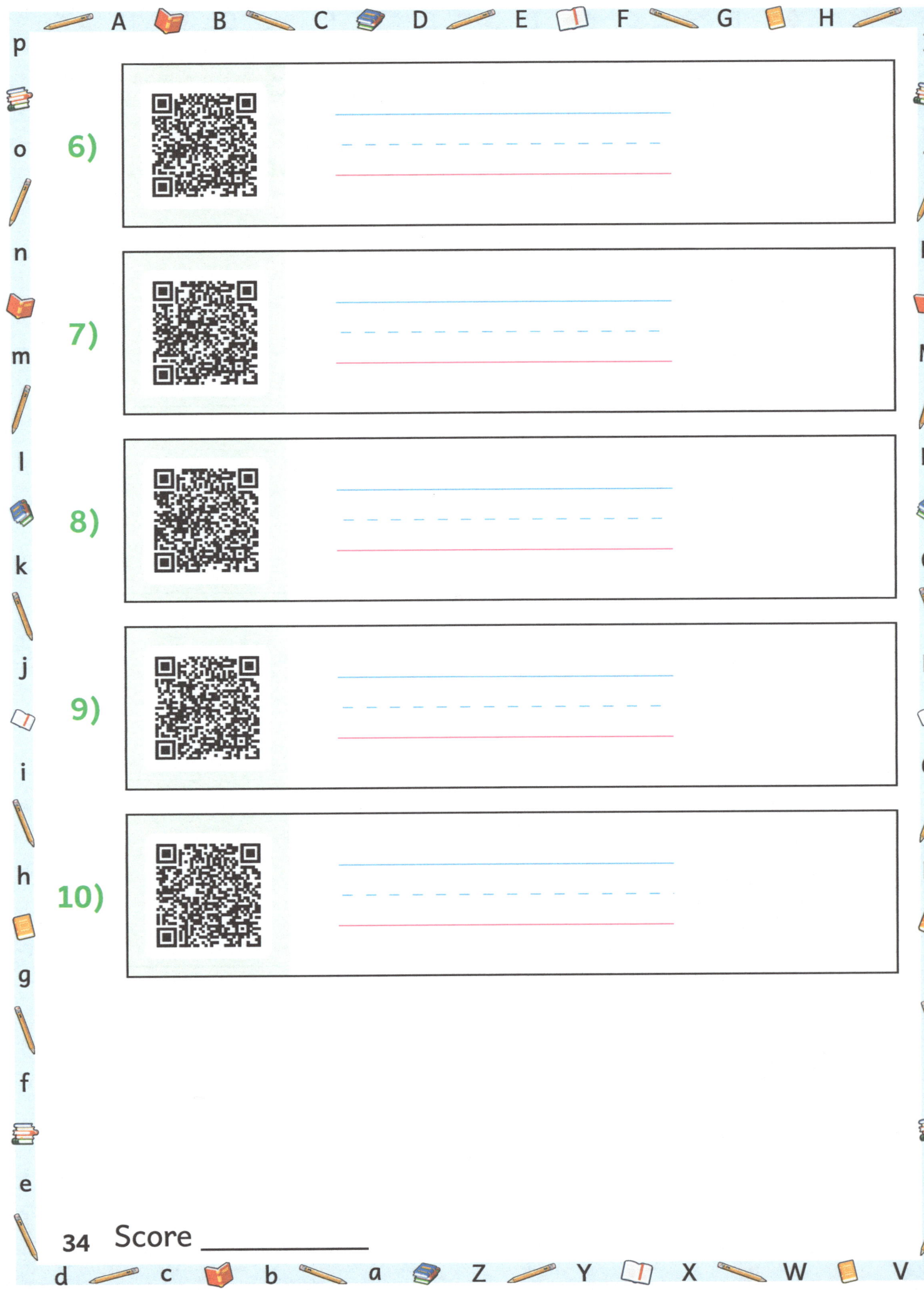

6)

7)

8)

9)

10)

Learn:

- Determine how to spell the final **j** sound.
- Spell and read words from List 14.

WRITING PHONOGRAM REVIEW

Listen to and write the phonograms.
Underline any multi-letter phonograms.

Spelling Rules

Ending **j** sound: Use **dge** to spell the **j** sound at the end of a one-syllable base word after one short vowel. Use **ge** after any other vowel or a consonant.

pl**edge**   st**age**   fri**nge**

Write the correct answers.
Add the ending letters for each word.

1)  ju _____

2)  smu _____

3)  spon _____

4)  pa _____

5)  fri _____

6)  lar _____

7)  ba _____

8)  lun _____

9)  char _____

Listen!

 **Circle the correct answers.**

| 10) | syllables | 1 | 2 | 3 | 4 |

| 11) | sounds | 1 | 2 | 3 | 4 |

 **Write and read.**

12) _____

 **Choose the correct answer.**

13) What is the syllable type?
- ○ closed
- ○ open
- ○ vowel team

Listen!

? Circle the correct answers.

14)	syllables	1	2	3	4

15)	sounds	1	2	3	4

✏ Write and read.

16) _____

? Choose the correct answer.

17) Which position is the vowel sound in?
- ○ beginning
- ○ middle
- ○ ending

Listen!

 **Circle the correct answers.**

18)	syllables	1	2	3	4

19)	sounds	1	2	3	4

Write and read.

20) _____

Choose the correct answer.

21) The vowel sound is ____.
- ○ long
- ○ short
- ○ r-controlled

 **Choose the correct answer.**

22) Which word begins with two consonant sounds?

○ dodge ○ edge ○ bridge

 **Circle the correct answers.**
Which picture describes the sentence?

23) The girl sat on the **edge** of her bed.

24) I made a **bridge** out of blocks.

25) The mouse ran quickly to **dodge** the cat.

SCORE CORRECT RESCORE

ACTIVITY: Writing Words

Read, trace, and write these words.

Read	Trace	Write
voice	voice	
were	were	
noise	noise	
please	please	
are	are	
leave	leave	
give	give	
done	done	
some	some	

Learn:

- Determine how to spell the final **ch** sound.

- Spell and read words from List 14.

WRITING PHONOGRAM REVIEW

Listen to and write the phonograms.
Underline any multi-letter phonograms.

Spelling Rules

Ending **ch** sound: Use **tch** to spell the **ch** sound at the end of a one-syllable base word after one short vowel. Use **ch** after any other vowel or a consonant.

sk**e**tch   p**ea**ch

 **Write the correct answers.**
Add the ending letters for each word.

1)

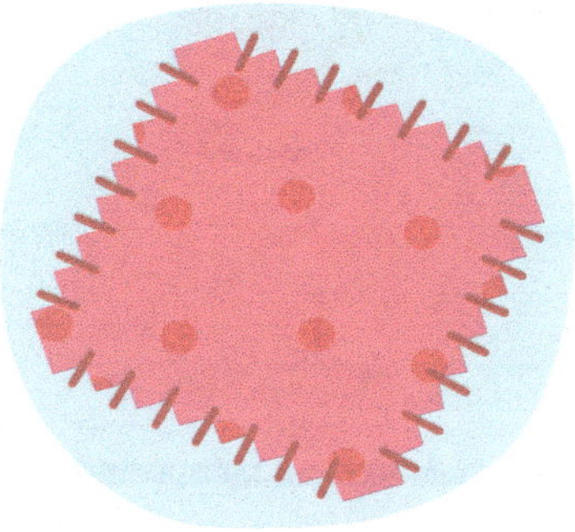

pa____

2)

bran____

3)

laun____

4)

cru____

5)

tea____

6)

i____

7)

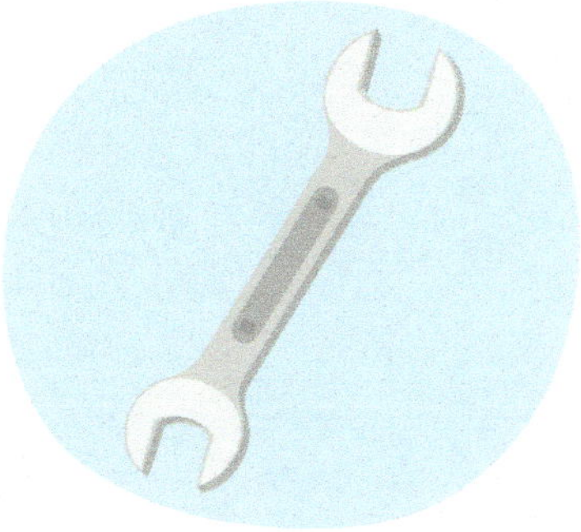

wren____

8)

stre____

9)

fe____

Listen!

? **Circle the correct answers.**

10) | syllables | 1 | 2 | 3 | 4 |

11) | sounds | 1 | 2 | 3 | 4 |

✏️ **Write and read.**

12) _____

? **Choose the correct answer.**

13) What is the syllable type?
- ○ vowel team
- ○ closed
- ○ open

Listen!

 **Circle the correct answers.**

14)	syllables	1	2	3	4

15)	sounds	1	2	3	4

 **Write and read.**

16) _____

 **Choose the correct answer.**

17) The vowel sound is ____.
- ○ short
- ○ long
- ○ r–controlled

Listen!

 **Circle the correct answers.**

18)	syllables	1	2	3	4

19)	sounds	1	2	3	4

 **Write and read.**

20) _____

 **Choose the correct answer.**

21) Which reading rule does this word follow?
   ○ 2nd sound of **c**
   ○ middle **s**
   ○ 1st sound of **c**

Listen!

 **Circle the correct answers.**

22)	syllables	1	2	3	4

23)	sounds	1	2	3	4

 **Write and read.**

24) _____

 **Choose the correct answer.**

25) How many consonant sounds are in the word?

○ 3

○ 1

○ 2

 **Choose the correct answers.**

26) Mark (☒) the TWO words that rhyme.

☐ pitch   ☐ match   ☐ catch

 **Write the correct answers.**
Sort the words in ABC order.

| pitch | match | lunch |

27) _____

28) _____

29) _____

 **Use the word in your own sentence.**

| catch |

30) _____

SCORE   CORRECT   RESCORE

50

Learn:

- Determine how to spell the final **k** sound.

- Spell and read words from List 14.

WRITING PHONOGRAM REVIEW

 **Listen to and write the phonograms.**
Underline any multi-letter phonograms.

Spelling Rules

Ending **k** sound: Use **ck** to spell the **k** sound at the end of a one-syllable base word after one short vowel. Use **ke** after one long vowel. Use **k** after any other vowel or a consonant.

sn**ack** c**a**k**e** f**or**k m**i**lk

1)

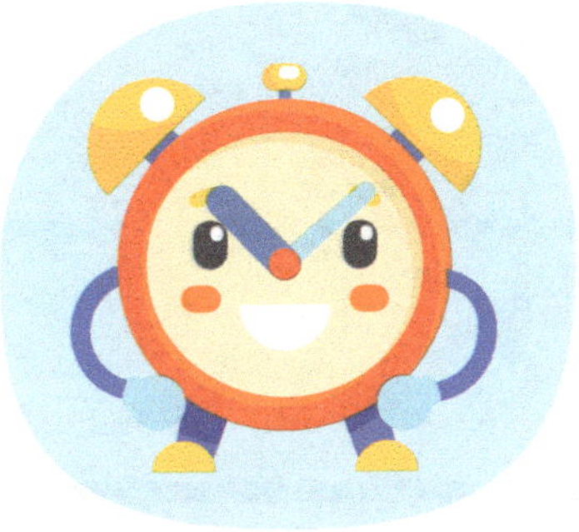

clo_____

2)

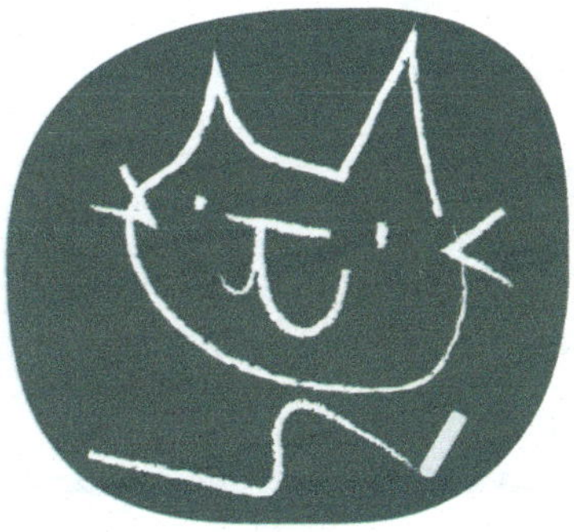

chal_____

3)

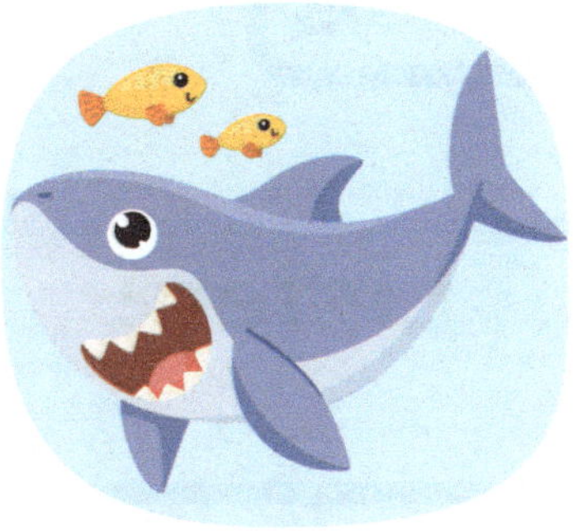

shar_____

4)

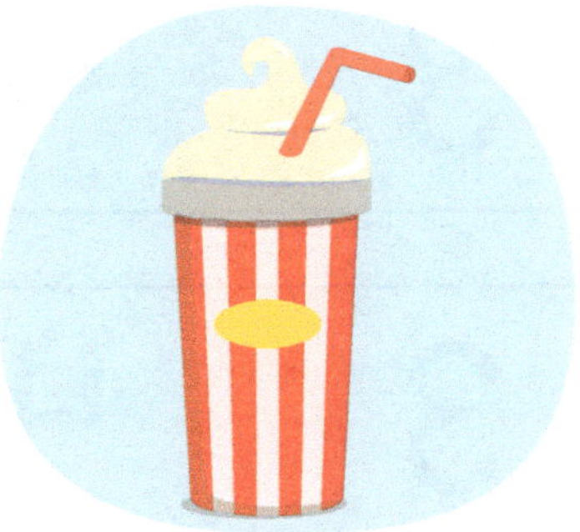

sha_____

5)

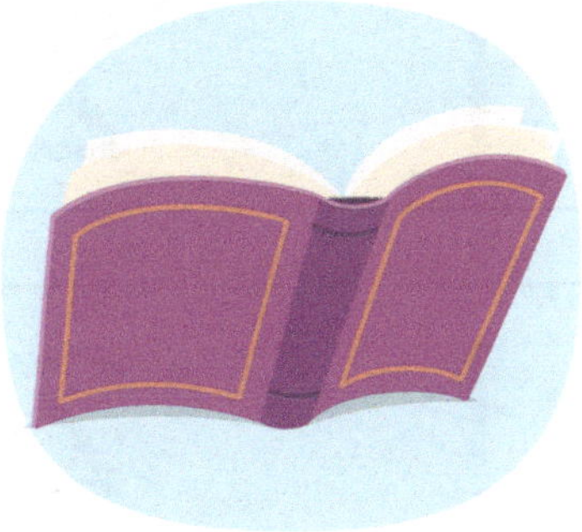

boo_____

6)

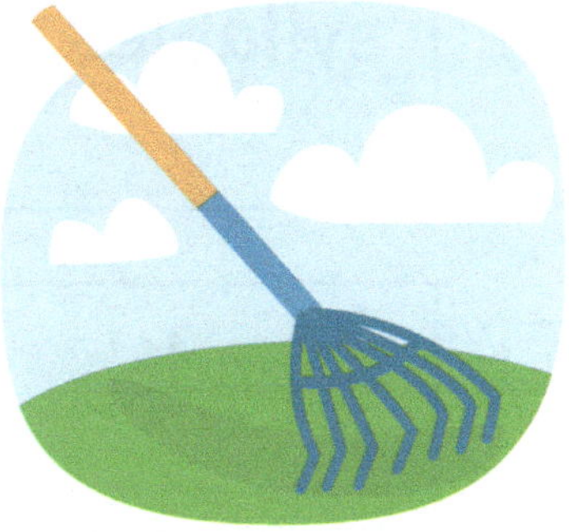

ra_____

7)

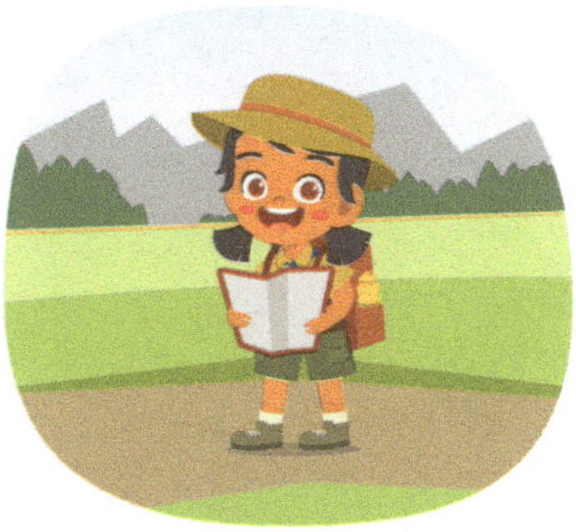

hi_____

8)

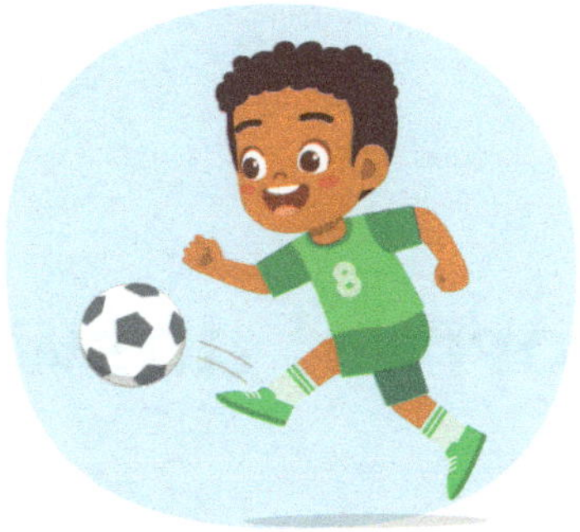

ki_____

9)

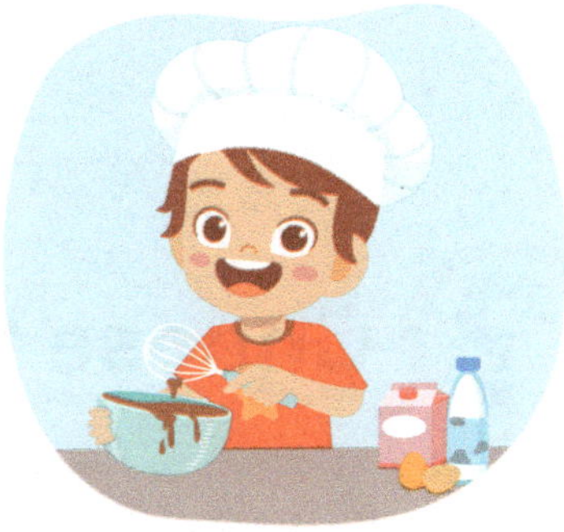

ba_____

53

Listen!

 **Circle the correct answers.**

| 10) | syllables | 1 | 2 | 3 | 4 |

| 11) | sounds | 1 | 2 | 3 | 4 |

 **Write and read.**

12) _____

 **Choose the correct answer.**

13) What is the syllable type?
   - ○ open
   - ○ VCe
   - ○ vowel team

 **Circle the correct answers.**

14) | syllables | 1 | 2 | 3 | 4 |

15) | sounds | 1 | 2 | 3 | 4 |

 **Write and read.**

16) _____

 **Choose the correct answer.**

17) Which reading rule does this word follow?
- ○ 3rd sound of **a**
- ○ **o** before **m**, **n**, or **v**
- ○ 3rd sound of **u**

Listen!

Circle the correct answers.

18)	syllables	1	2	3	4

19)	sounds	1	2	3	4

Write and read.

20) _____

Choose the correct answer.

21) What is the syllable type?

  ○ closed

  ○ open

  ○ vowel team

 **Choose the correct answer.**

22) Which word has a silent final **e**?
- ○ look
- ○ bike
- ○ walk

 **Write the correct answers.**
Complete the sentences.

bike	walk	look

23) Let's go _____ at the puppies.

24) It is a short _____ down the street.

25) You can ride your _____ if you want.

ACTIVITY: Writing Words

Read, trace, and write these words.

Read	Trace	Write
bridge	bridge	
edge	edge	
dodge	dodge	
pitch	pitch	
match	match	
catch	catch	
lunch	lunch	
bike	bike	
walk	walk	

PHONOGRAM REVIEW

 **Listen to and circle the correct phonograms.**

1)  d   t   n

2)  f   ph   v

3)  ey   ee   ea

4)  oa   oo   oe

5)  th   sh   ch

6) gn   n   kn

7) ur   ar   ear

8) e   o   u

9) n   p   m

10) ci   si   sh

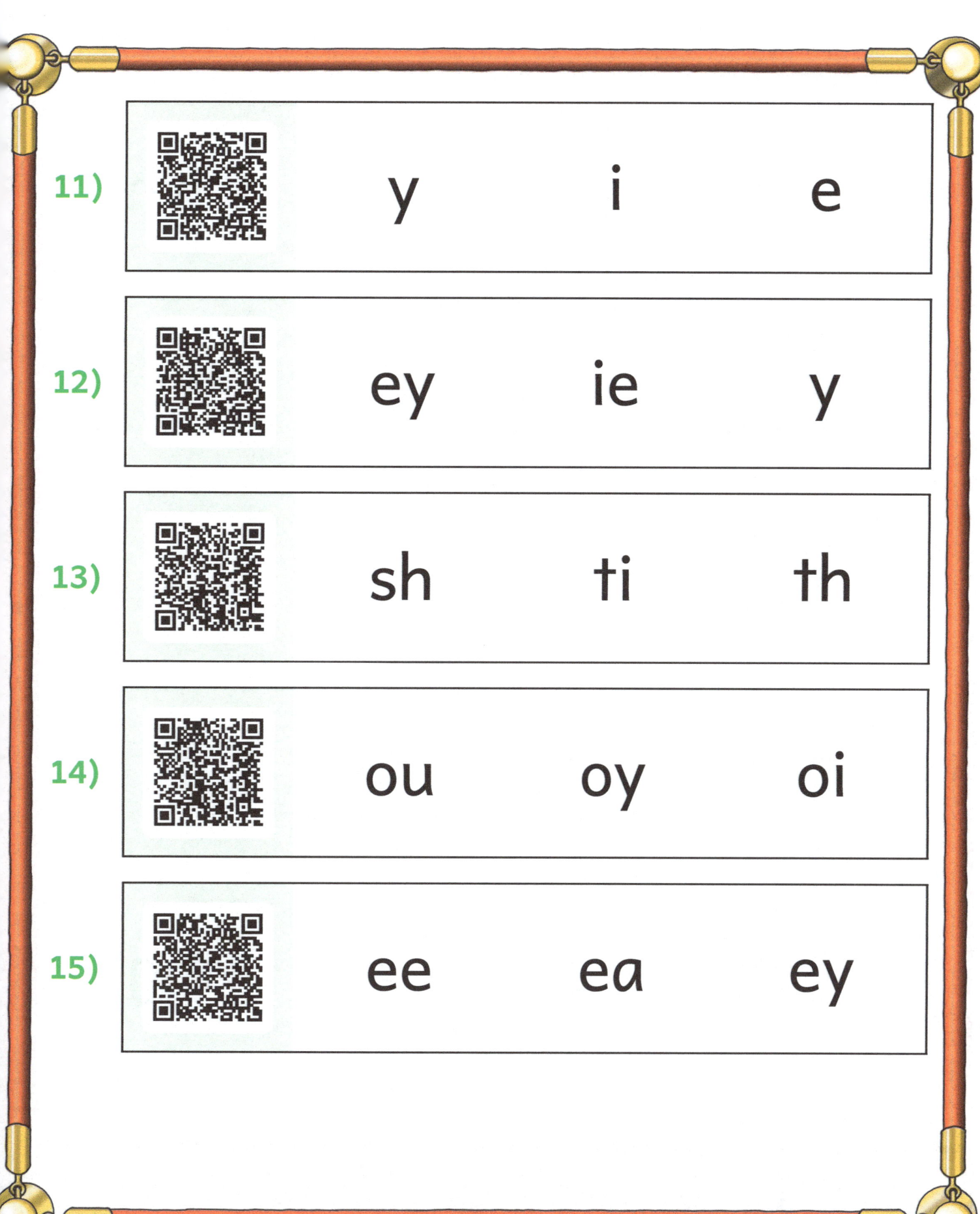

11) y   i   e

12) ey   ie   y

13) sh   ti   th

14) ou   oy   oi

15) ee   ea   ey

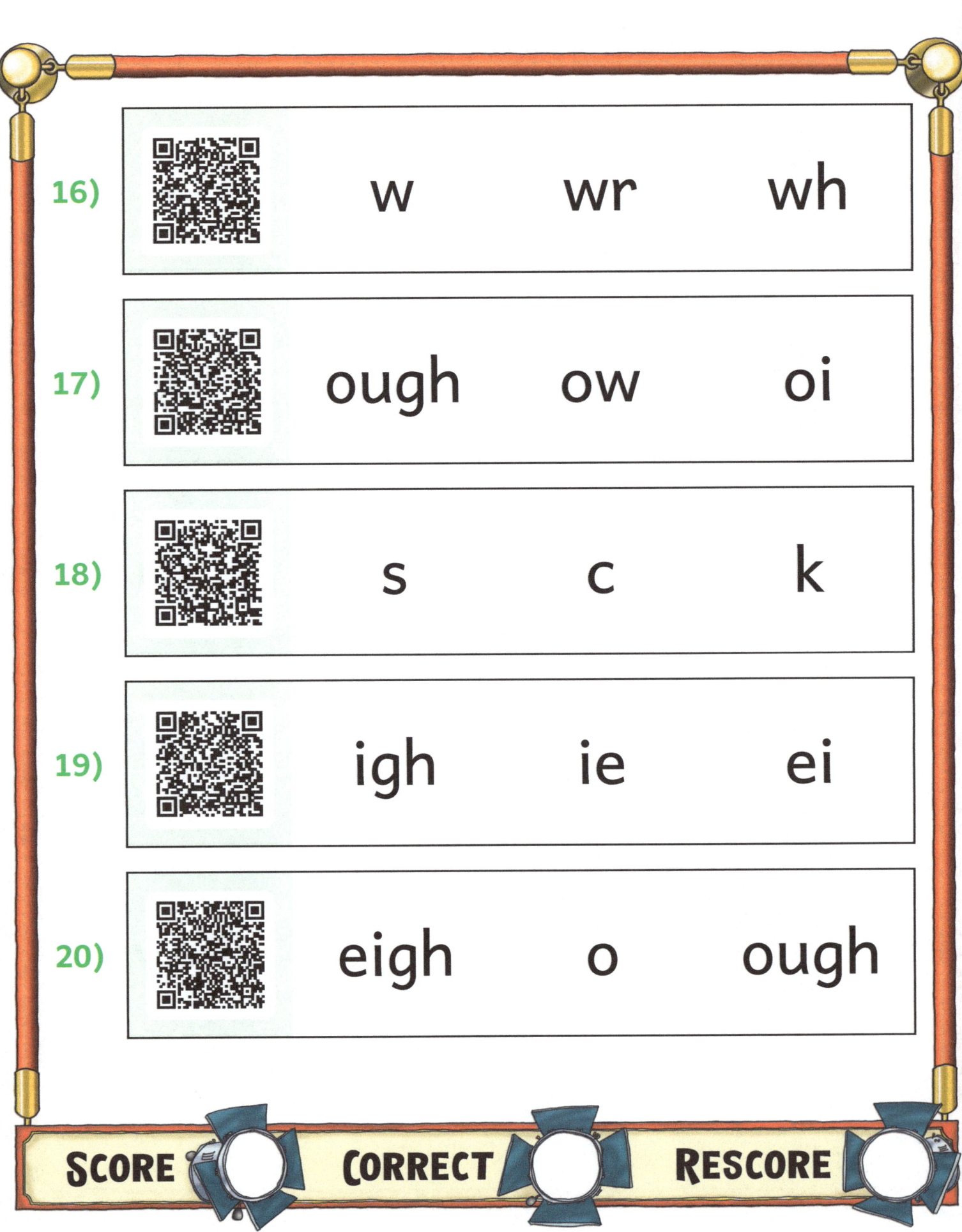

16) w   wr   wh

17) ough   ow   oi

18) s   c   k

19) igh   ie   ei

20) eigh   o   ough

SCORE   CORRECT   RESCORE

Write the correct answers.
Sort the words in ABC order. You will need to use the second letter for some words.

look	bike	match	lunch	bridge
catch	edge	dodge	walk	pitch

1) _____

2) _____

3) _____

4) _____

5) _____

6) _____

7) _____

8) _____

9) _____

10) _____

READER 21: "The Big Race"

This Reader has the tricky word *shoe*. The vowel team **oe** does not make its usual sound. It makes the second sound of **oo**. It only does this in one other word: *canoe*.

Tricky Word
shoe

sh**oe**

can**oe**

 **Circle the words that rhyme with *shoe*.**

clue   go   the   to

you   may   new   line

Reader 21
The Big Race

 **Choose the correct answers.**

1) Which two pals were racing?
- ○ Bix and Ottie
- ○ Ottie and Kit
- ○ Kit and Bix

2) What did the racers have to do with the shoes?
- ○ catch them
- ○ match them
- ○ dodge them

3) Who won the race?
- ○ Bix
- ○ Ottie
- ○ Kit

Phonogram Test 26

Listen to and write the correct phonograms.
Underline any multi-letter phonograms.

1)

2)

3)

4)

5)

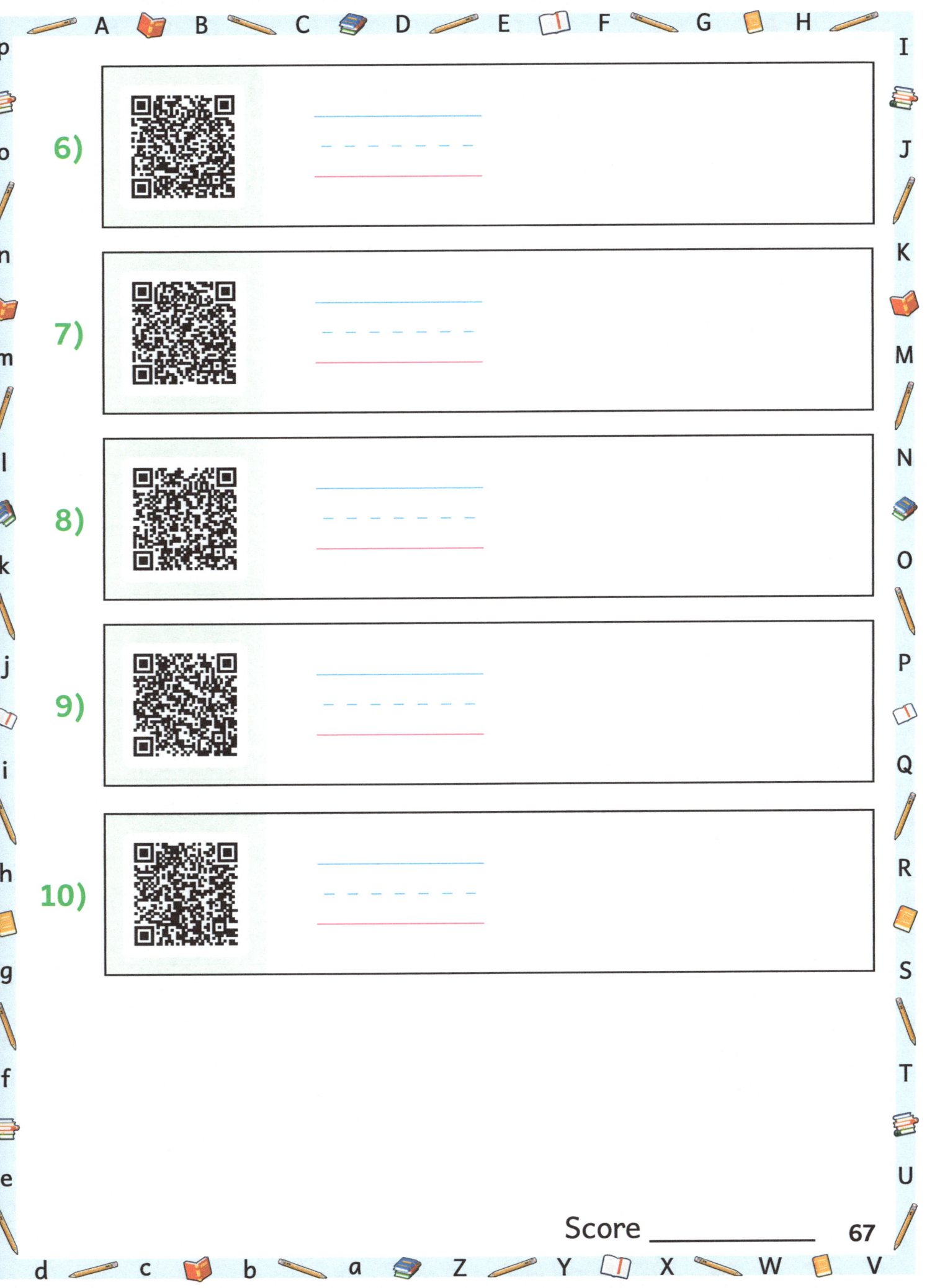

Spelling Test List 14

Listen to and write the spelling words.

1)

2)

3)

4)

5)

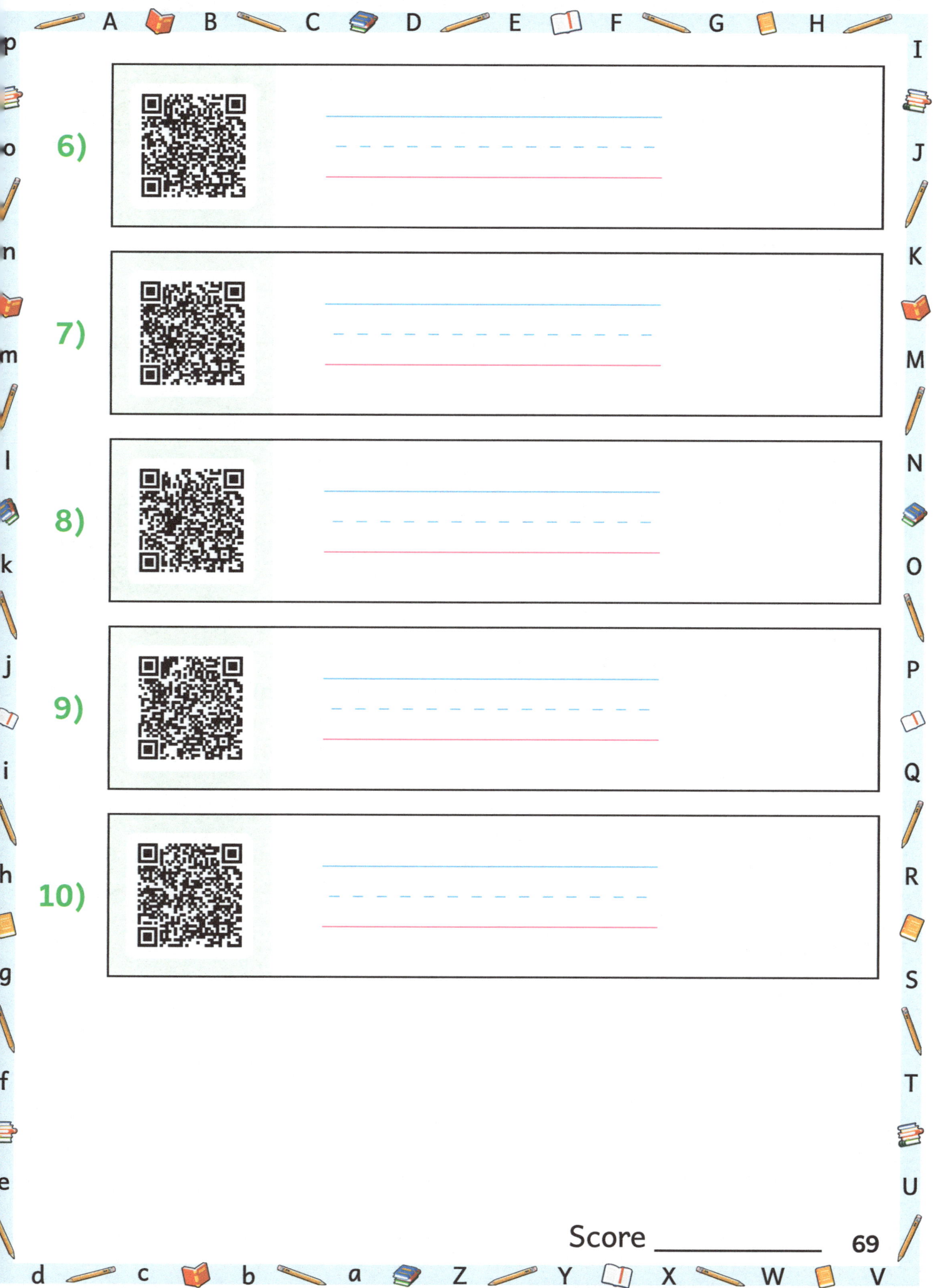

6)

7)

8)

9)

10)

Score _____ 69

7. SPELLING LIST 15: Part 1

Learn:

- Identify words with suffix **s.**
- Spell and read words from List 15.

WRITING PHONOGRAM REVIEW

Listen to and write the phonograms.
Underline any multi-letter phonograms.

WORKING WITH WORDS

Spelling List 15 has words with suffixes. Suffixes let us change the way we use a base word. The words in this Lesson have suffix **s**.

Suffix **s**
Makes nouns plural
Makes present-tense verbs agree with singular subjects

Three star**s** shine.

A star shine**s**.

Circle the correct answers.
Which word in each row uses suffix s?

1)	grass	storms	us
2)	nose	kiss	lips
3)	items	dress	chess
4)	rinse	pans	glass
5)	use	pies	cheese
6)	goose	has	eggs
7)	bus	roads	purse
8)	seeds	vase	moss

Write the correct answers.
Write the first letter from each answer above on the puzzle lines below.

9) What do you call two banana peels?

a pair of ____ ____ ____ ____ ____ ____ ____ ____

                1   2   3   4   5   6   7   8

 **Circle the correct answers.**

10)	syllables	1	2	3	4

11)	sounds	1	2	3	4

 **Write and read.**

12) _____

 **Choose the correct answer.**

13) What is the syllable type?
- ○ r-controlled
- ○ open
- ○ vowel team

Listen!

? **Circle the correct answers.**

14) | syllables | 1 | 2 | 3 | 4 |

15) | sounds | 1 | 2 | 3 | 4 |

✏️ **Write and read.**

16) _____

? **Choose the correct answer.**

17) Which spelling rule does this word follow?
- ○ floss rule
- ○ ending **ck**
- ○ ending **j** sound

 **Circle the correct answers.**

18)	syllables	1	2	3	4

19)	sounds	1	2	3	4

 **Write and read.**

20) _____

 **Choose the correct answer.**

21) What is the syllable type?
- ○ closed
- ○ open
- ○ vowel team

 **Choose the correct answer.**

22) Which word ends with an unvoiced **s**?

 ○ socks   ○ arms   ○ mugs

 **Circle the correct answers.**
Which picture describes the sentence?

23) My coat is too short for my **arms**.

24) James is wearing blue **socks**.

25) All of the **mugs** are broken.

SCORE   CORRECT   RESCORE

Learn:

- Determine when to use suffix **s** and **es**.

- Spell and read words from List 15.

WRITING PHONOGRAM REVIEW

 **Listen to and write the phonograms.**
Underline any multi-letter phonograms.

WORKING WITH WORDS

Spelling Rules

Suffix **es**: Use suffix **es** for suffix **s** when a base word ends with **s**, **x**, **z**, **ch**, or **sh**.

hi**sses**   fo**xes**   bu**zzes**   bran**ches**   bu**shes**

 **Write the correct answers.**
Add the suffix to the end of each word.

1)

box _____

2)

wink _____

3)

miss _____

4)

chair _____

5)

press _____

6)

watch _____

7)

read _____

8)

brush _____

9)

push _____

Listen!

 **Circle the correct answer.**

10) | syllables | 1 2 3 4 |

 **Circle the correct answers.**
Then, write each part of the word.

11) | base word |
| sounds | 1 2 3 4 |

12) | suffix |
| sounds | 1 2 3 4 |

✏️ **Write and read.**

13) _____

Listen!

 **Circle the correct answer.**

14) | syllables | 1 | 2 | 3 | 4 |

 **Circle the correct answers.**
Then, write each part of the word.

15) | base word |
| sounds | 1 2 3 4 |

16) | suffix |
| sounds | 1 2 3 4 |

 **Write and read.**

17) _____

Listen!

 **Circle the correct answer.**

18) | syllables | 1   2   3   4 |

 **Circle the correct answers.**
Then, write each part of the word.

19)
base word	
sounds	1 2 3 4

20)
suffix	
sounds	1 2 3 4

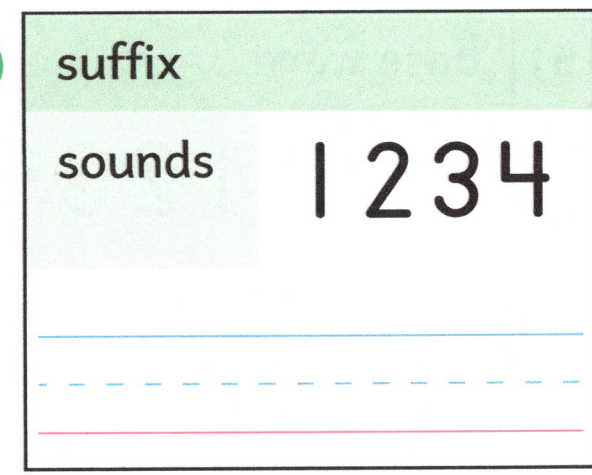 **Write and read.**

21) _____

Listen!

? **Circle the correct answer.**

22) | syllables | 1 2 3 4 |

? **Circle the correct answers.**
Then, write each part of the word.

23) base word

sounds 1 2 3 4

_____

24) suffix

sounds 1 2 3 4

_____

✏️ **Write and read.**

25) _____

? Choose the correct answers.

26) Mark (☒) TWO words that have a consonant digraph.

☐ lunches   ☐ buses   ☐ wishes

✏ Write the correct answers.
Sort the words in ABC order.

lunches	wishes	fixes

27) _____

28) _____

29) _____

✏ Use the word in your own sentence.

buses

30) _____

SCORE   CORRECT   RESCORE

Learn:

- Add suffixes **ing** and **ed** to base words.

- Spell and read words from List 15.

WRITING PHONOGRAM REVIEW

 **Listen to and write the phonograms.**
Underline any multi-letter phonograms.

WORKING WITH WORDS

Suffix ing

Says a verb is happening now

Always has a vowel sound

Today we are learn**ing**, ask**ing**, and count**ing**.

Suffix ed

Says a verb happened in the past

Only has a vowel sound after the letters **d** or **t**

Today we learn**ed**, ask**ed**, and count**ed**.

Write the correct answers.

Write each base word with each suffix.
Circle the words that have two syllables.

Base Word	Suffix ing	Suffix ed
1) yawn		
2) look		
3) fold		
4) show		
5) count		

Listen!

 **Circle the correct answer.**

6) | syllables | 1 2 3 4 |

 **Circle the correct answers.**
Then, write each part of the word.

7) base word
sounds 1 2 3 4

_____

8) suffix
sounds 1 2 3 4

_____

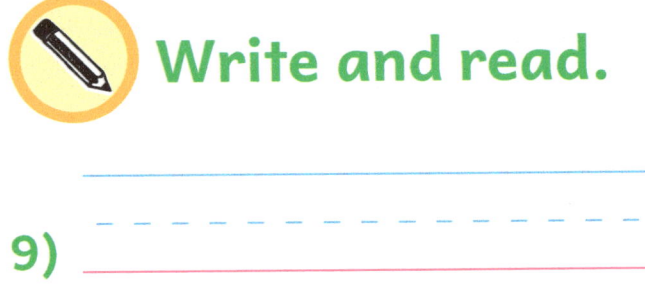 **Write and read.**

9) _____

Listen!

 **Circle the correct answers.**

| 10) | syllables | 1 | 2 | 3 | 4 | 5 |

| 11) | sounds | 1 | 2 | 3 | 4 | 5 |

 **Write and read.**

12) _____

 **Choose the correct answer.**

13) What is the base word?
- ○ jumpe
- ○ jump
- ○ jum

Listen!

 **Circle the correct answer.**

14) | syllables | 1   2   3   4 |

 **Circle the correct answers.**
Then, write each part of the word.

15) | base word |
| sounds | 1 2 3 4 |

16) | suffix |
| sounds | 1 2 3 4 |

Write and read.

17) _____

90

 **Choose the correct answers.**

18) Mark (☒) TWO words that are in the past tense.

☐ jumped

☐ lifted

☐ going

 **Write the correct answers.**
Complete the sentences.

jumped	lifted	going

19) My dad told me that we are _____ to the beach!

20) I was so happy that I _____ in the air and cheered.

21) We walked outside, and I _____ my hand to block the sun.

PHONOGRAM REVIEW

Listen to and circle the correct phonograms.

1) wh   h   t

2) b   d   p

3) a   i   y

4) ear   or   wor

5) eigh   ay   ea

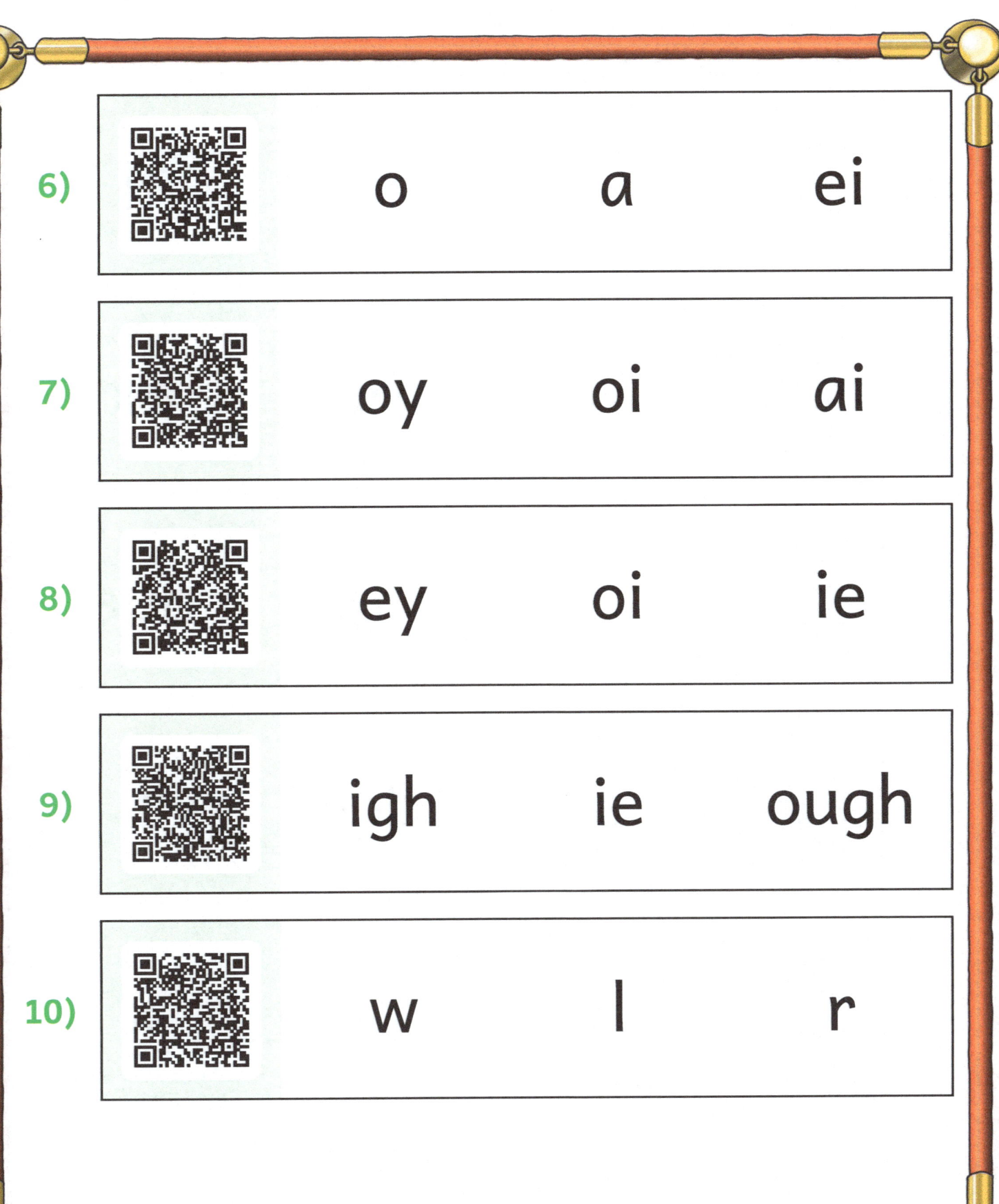

6) o   a   ei

7) oy   oi   ai

8) ey   oi   ie

9) igh   ie   ough

10) w   l   r

11) t   sh   ti

12) m   gn   nk

13) x   g   dge

14) ed   dge   t

15) v   ph   x

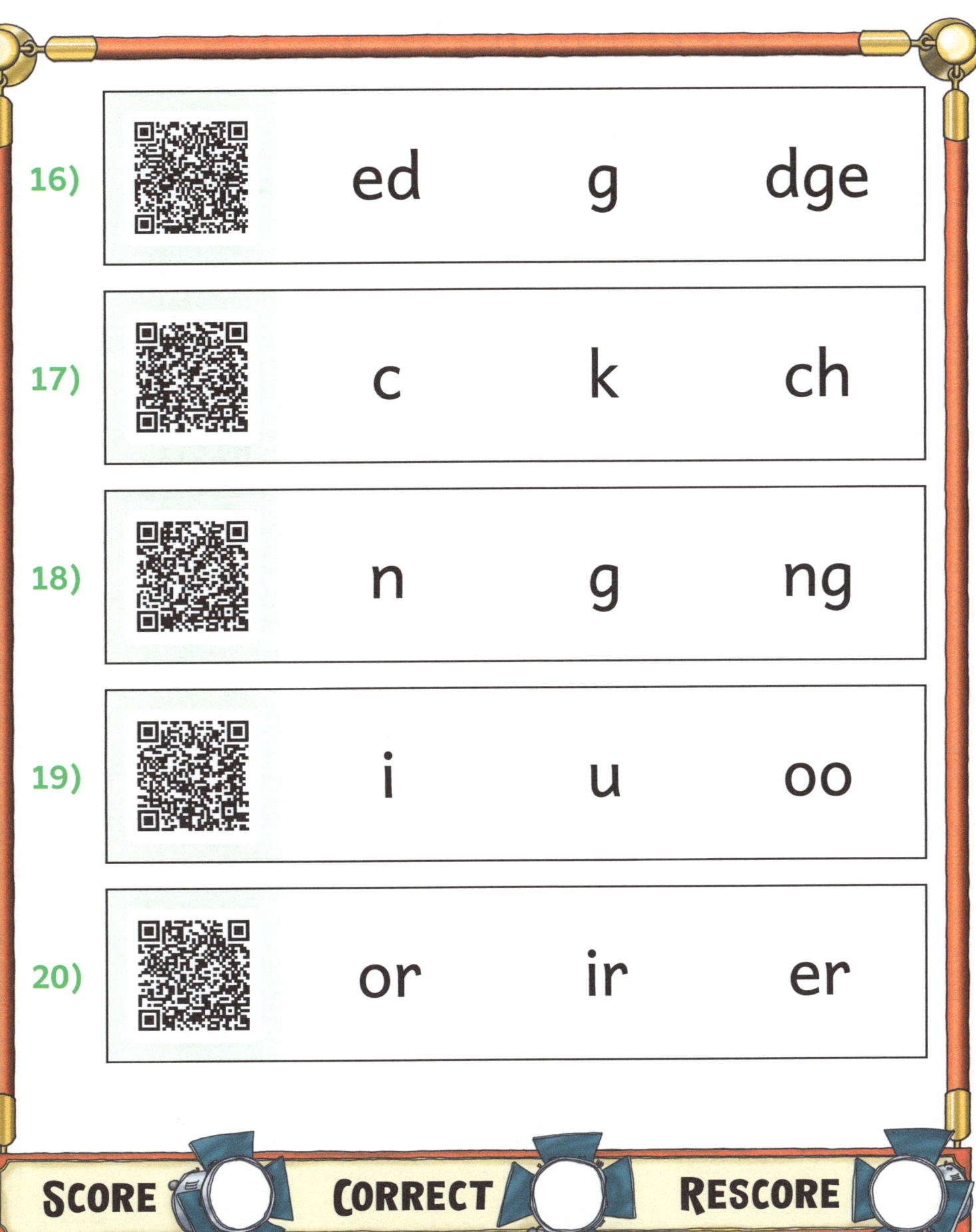

16) ed   g   dge

17) c   k   ch

18) n   g   ng

19) i   u   oo

20) or   ir   er

SCORE   CORRECT   RESCORE

SPELLING LIST 15 REVIEW

 **Write the correct answers.**
Sort the words by the number of syllables.

> mugs   jumped   wishes   buses   socks
> arms   lifted   lunches   going   fixes

1) **1 Syllable**

2) **2 Syllables**

READER 22: "Meg and the Fighting Fish"

This Reader has the tricky word *built*. It is the past tense form of *build*. The vowel team **ui** does not make its usual sound. It makes the short **i** sound.

Tricky Word
bu**i**lt

Listen to the forms of the word *build* in this sentence.

When we are done **building** this **building**, we will **build** the biggest **building** that has ever been **built**!

Write the correct answers.
Complete the sentences.

build   building   built

1) Last year, we _____ a birdhouse for our yard.

2) Now, we are _____ a doghouse for Rover.

3) Next, I want to _____ a tree house for me!

Reader 22
Meg and the Fighting Fish

 **Choose the correct answers.**

4) What keeps Quack from going fishing?
- ○ He is afraid of fish.
- ○ He needs to do his homework.
- ○ He has to take the mail.

5) What did Bix build?
- ○ a new dock
- ○ chairs for the pals
- ○ the fishing rods

6) What did Meg do with the fish?
- ○ put it in a tank at home
- ○ swam with it
- ○ let it go back in the water

Phonogram Test 27

Listen to and write the correct phonograms.
Underline any multi-letter phonograms.

1)

2)

3)

4)

5)

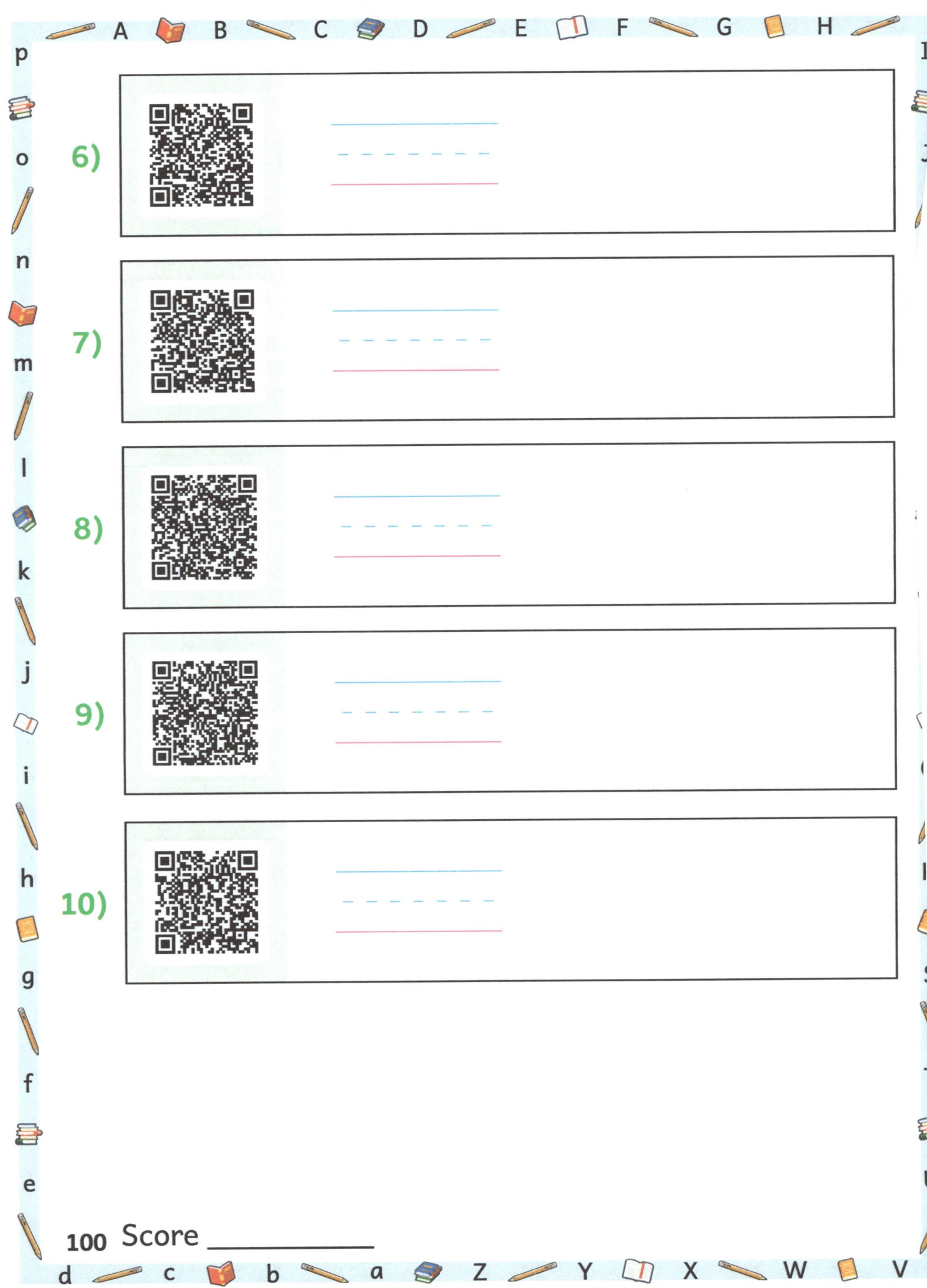

Score _____

Spelling Test List 15

Listen to and write the spelling words.

1)

2)

3)

4)

5)

6)

7)

8)

9)

10)